... for those domestic
lacunae!
With much love from
the Oblong girls x x

October 2007

Practical Know-how
in the Home

SIMON &
SCHUSTER

LONDON • NEW YORK • SYDNEY • TORONTO

First published in Great Britain by
Simon & Schuster UK Ltd 2007
A CBS Company

Copyright © this compilation WI Enterprises Ltd, 2007
All rights reserved.
Illustrations copyright © Jane Norman 2007

ISBN 1 8473 70047

Simon and Schuster UK Ltd
Africa House
64–78 Kingsway
London WC2B 6AH

1 3 5 7 9 10 8 6 4 2

Design and illustrations by Jane Norman
Jacket design by Kari Brownlie
Printed and bound in China

Contents

Introduction

The Women's Institute championed an eco-friendly approach to keeping our homes clean long before it became fashionable. This little book suggests a range of inexpensive, time-tested products that will tackle household jobs efficiently. There's excellent advice on stain removal for those inevitable spillages, plus tips on removing marks from wooden furniture. And did you know that an ice cube gets rid of a dent in the carpet or talcum powder can sort out squeaky floorboards? With additional tips on caring for clothes, money-saving advice and apposite quotations from famous names, this is a fascinating book you shouldn't be without.

" The amount of women in London who flirt with their own husbands is perfectly scandalous. It looks so bad. It is simply washing one's clean linen in public."

Oscar Wilde, 1854–1900

Stains and Washing Know-how

To keep whites white

Put 2 tablespoons of washing soda in the washing powder compartment of the machine with your chosen detergent and wash as normal.

To remove grease marks

Soak greasy clothes overnight in a strong
solution of 1 cup washing soda to 600 ml
(1 pint) water. Drain, squeeze lightly and
then wash the clothes as normal.

Washing delicate lace underwear and tights

Put them in an old pillowcase and
machine wash as normal.

" I think if you've got a T-shirt with a bloodstain all over it, maybe laundry isn't your biggest problem. Maybe you should get rid of the body before you do the wash. "

Jerry Seinfeld, b. 1954

Faded colours?

Sometimes fading is the result of a build up of washing powder within the fabric. Rinsing faded clothes in water with a good dash of white vinegar added can get rid of the soap and bring the colour back. The same treatment can work on black clothes that have developed a whitish bloom. Wash normally afterwards to freshen the clothes.

❋

" *They tend to come out a colour called 'Pants left in wash'* **"**

Eddie Izzard, b. 1962

To make worn towels fluffy

Soak them overnight in cold water with a cup of washing soda added. Do this in a bucket or use the soak cycle of the washing machine. Add detergent and wash as normal the next day. Wash towels in the hottest wash.

To remove grease stains from suede

Try rubbing with a little neat white vinegar on
a soft cloth. Allow it to dry in sunlight
and brush to restore.

Red wine, coffee and tea

Soda water will remove all of these, especially
if you act immediately. Lift any solid particles
from the surface. Pour soda water on to the
stain and blot with a dry cloth or disposable
cloth and then wash as normal.

❝ *We should all do what, in the long run, gives us joy, even if it is only picking grapes or sorting the laundry.* **❞**

E.B White, 1899–1985

" *Lately I've been looking at old-fashioned plaids, fingering starched white collars, wondering whether there's a way to get them really white again.* **"**

John Ashbery, b.1927

Dirty shirt collars and lipstick stains

Rub a small amount of pale-coloured shampoo into the collar or lipstick mark before washing. Shampoo is designed to dissolve body oils.

Heavy stains on cotton and linen

Stains such as blood, grease, ink, tea and coffee can be sprayed directly with liquid soda crystals, or soaked overnight in a strong solution of washing soda. Allow 1 cup soda to 600 ml (1 pint) water. Wash as normal afterwards.

❋

" *Wash your soiled linen in private.* **"**

Napoleon Bonaparte, 1769–1821

To remove candle wax from clothes

Chip off as much wax as you can.
Protect the ironing board with a clean old cloth.
Place the stained fabric on top and lay a sheet
of brown paper over the mark. Brown paper
bags are good, but make sure there is no print
on them. Iron the paper using a medium heat,
without steam, and you'll find that the wax will
melt into the paper. Move the paper as it
absorbs the wax, so that you are ironing a
clean area each time.

Deodorant stains

Sponge white vinegar onto the stain or rub with a cut lemon and leave for 30 minutes. Wash the item in the hottest wash that is safe for the fabric (check the care label).

Underarm stain on cotton clothing

Dissolve 8–10 aspirins in a cup of warm water.
Soak the underarm area of the garment in
this for 30 minutes and then wash as normal.
Be sure to throw the aspirin water
away immediately.

To remove chewing gum

Start by putting the garment into a plastic bag and placing it in the freezer overnight. Remove from the freezer and immediately scrape off as much gum as you can with a blunt knife. Then rub in a little white vinegar and washing-up liquid and wash as normal.

Automatic washing machines: please remove
all your clothes when the light goes out.

Sign in laundromat

" Beautiful furniture gives us something to live up to. All designed objects are propaganda for a way of life."

Alain de Botton, b. 1969

Furniture

Removing a water or heat mark from wood

Try massaging a small amount of mayonnaise
into the stain. Leave overnight before wiping it
off. You can also use butter or margarine,
which is less smelly!

To clean cane and wicker furniture

Make up a solution of ½ cup washing soda to 600 ml (1 pint) warm water to wipe over the furniture. The soda hardens the cane and tightens sagging seats.

Get rid of musty smells in wooden wardrobes and chests

Put a slice of white bread in a bowl and pour in enough white vinegar to cover the bread. Stand the bowl inside the closed furniture for 24 hours, or longer if the smell is still there.

Removing old polish and dirt from furniture

Use a cloth wrung out in warm water, mixed with 1 tablespoon of malt vinegar to 600 ml (1 pint) water. Allow this to dry and then re-polish. This mixture can also be used to remove the build up of spray polish on any type of surface.

*

Shin: Device for finding furniture in the dark.

Anon.

"*A house that does not have one worn, comfy chair in it is soulless.***"**

May Sarton, 1912–1995

Maintaining leather furniture

Avoid positioning leather furniture in direct sunlight or near heat sources. Try to remove spots and spills as soon as they happen. Blot any excess liquid with a clean cloth or sponge, dry with a towel and allow to air dry. Don't apply water to an oily or greasy mark; just wipe off any excess with a clean, dry cloth and leave. Don't use saddle soap or anything abrasive on leather.

To make sure a sofa wears evenly

Rotate the cushions as often as you can,
pulling them out, turning them over
and repositioning them.

Moving heavy furniture

Place some really thick polythene (sacks are
suitable) under each leg or corner. You will
then be able to slide the furniture into
position quite easily.

Furniture

"We had gay burglars the other night. They broke in and rearranged the furniture."

Robin Williams, b.1952

" Dust is a protective coating
for fine furniture. "

Mario Buatta, b.1935

Best care for wooden furniture

Do not overuse spray polish (containing silicone) as it will build up on the surface and become streaky and smeary. Dust once a week and polish occasionally: use bees' wax three to four times a year. Leave it on for 30 minutes or so to give it a chance to sink into the wood. Buff with a soft duster.

*" The wise man sits on the
hole in his carpet "*

Persian proverb

Fixtures and Fittings

To remove a dent in a carpet

This simple technique really does work.
Place an ice cube, or a tablespoon of cold
water, in the dent: as the carpet pile slowly
dries it will spring back to life.

To absorb musty carpet smells

Try mixing bicarbonate of soda with a few broken cloves; sprinkle on the carpet and leave overnight. Vacuum in the morning to leave the carpet smelling fresh.

✳

❝ *The chance of the bread falling with the buttered side down is directly proportional to the cost of the carpet* **❞**

Anon.

Removing wine, tea and coffee stains from carpets

Pour or spray soda water over the mark as quickly as possible. Blot with a dry or disposable cloth. Don't be afraid to wet the carpet – it goes through countless dippings in water during manufacture.

Removing grease spots from wallpaper

Make a paste of cornflour and water. Apply the paste to the spot and allow it to dry, then gently brush off.

To remove marks from non-washable wallpaper

Rub a scrunched up piece of white bread over the spots. You may have to repeat this a few times, but it does work.

❝ Cleaning is the best thing for the human mind and body. Seeing all the dirt being sucked up is an instant gratification!❞

Helena Christensen, b.1968

Cleaning windows

Start by washing dirty windows with a bucket
of warm water with a good squirt of washing-up
liquid added. Dry with a chamois or an old linen
tea towel. Make up a mixture of 2 tablespoons
of white vinegar to 600 ml (1 pint) water in a
spray bottle. Spray over windows and polish or
buff them dry with paper towels, a lint-free rag
or an old linen tea towel; or try using an inky
newspaper (the print in the paper makes
the windows shine).

"*Law of Window Cleaning:*
It's on the other side"

Anon.

Sticky sash windows

Try rubbing a candle repeatedly over the
touching surfaces. If sticking continues check
for a build of paint, in which case you need to
strip back to the wood and redecorate. If damp
is the issue, leave to dry out, strip back to the
wood and decorate to stop damp
being absorbed.

" *Life is denied by lack of attention,*

whether it be to cleaning windows

or trying to write a masterpiece. **"**

Nadia Boulanger, 1887–1979

Squeaky floorboards?

Try sprinkling talcum powder between
the floorboards.

✳

" The door to happiness opens outward."

Anon.

Hard to shut doors

Doors that are hard to keep shut often have
hinges that are set too deep in the door or
frame. Raise them by putting strips of
cardboard underneath. If screw heads protrude
and stop hinges closing properly, you may have
to fit smaller screws that sit well
into the hinges.

To loosen sticking locks

Try squirting a little WD40 into the latch,
bolt holes and keyhole using the straw-
type applicator.

To clean painted and UVPC window frames

Wipe down regularly with a solution of ½ cup
washing soda to 600 ml (1 pint) water.
Liquid soda is available as an alternative to
soda crystals.

❝ *A soulmate is someone who has locks that fit our keys, and keys to fit our locks.* **❞**

Richard Bach, b1936

"I'm a lousy cook but one helluva cleaning lady."

Maureen O'Hara, b.1920

To stop the bathroom mirror steaming up

Rub a few drops of shampoo, shaving cream or washing-up liquid on the glass with a clean, dry cloth.

> *"Rust consumes iron and envy consumes itself."*

Danish proverb

Crockery and Cutlery

To clean a rusty knife

Peel a large onion and stick the rusty part of
the knife into it. Move the blade backwards and
forwards several times to help the
onion juice do its work.

To remove rust from work surfaces

This is useful for Formica and plastic laminates.
Make a paste of cream of tartar (from the
baking section of shops) and fresh lemon juice.
Apply the paste to the rust spot and leave for
about 30 minutes. Scrub the surface
with a scourer and rinse.

To remove tea or coffee stains from cups and mugs

Using kitchen towel, rub the stained areas with a little salt or bicarbonate of soda. Alternatively, soak for an hour or overnight in a solution of washing soda, using 1 cup soda to 600ml (1 pint) water. Wash and rinse the china thoroughly.

To clean vases, glass decanters and scent bottles

Fill with warm water and pop in 1–2 denture cleaning tablets. Leave overnight and you will be able to rinse the dirt and stains away. Repeat the process to remove more stubborn marks.

Looking after glasses

Stand freshly washed glasses on a clean linen
tea towel to avoid slipping and chipping.
To make glass really sparkly and clean, add a
splash of vinegar to the final rinsing water.

To clean up broken glass

A thick slice of bread will pick up all the little
broken shards of glass that scatter everywhere.
Be careful, though, and do not turn the slice
of bread over.

To separate stacked glasses
without breaking them

Stand the bottom glass in hot water (not
boiling) and pour cold water into the top glass.
Twist the glasses very lightly and you should
be able to pull them apart easily.

“ *Friendship is like a glass ornament, once it is broken it can rarely be put back together exactly the same way.* **”**

Anon.

Chipped drinking glasses

There are companies that will regrind chipped glasses. This is worthwhile for good quality glassware – particularly cut glass. Ask in the china and glassware department of a large store to find out if they offer this service.

❝ *Is the glass half full, or half empty?*
It depends on whether you're
pouring, or drinking. **❞**

Bill Cosby, b.1937

✳

❝ *A few months ago they (the Duffers)*
were all for washing up the plates
and knives before dinner: they said
it saved time afterwards... **❞**

C.S Lewis, 1898–1963

*" Fewer and fewer Americans possess objects
that have a patina, old furniture,
grandparents pots and pans/the used things,
warm with generations of human touch,
essential to a human landscape."*

Susan Sontag, 1933–2004

Pots, Pans and Kitchen Accessories

Removing burnt-on food from roasting tins and pans

Fill the tin or pan with hot water and add 2–3 tablespoons of washing soda. Leave to soak overnight, then wash and rinse.

Dealing with a warped wooden bread board

Try placing it on a flat surface, warped side down, and covering it with a wet tea towel. Leave for at least 24 hours.

To remove stains from a non-stick cooking pan

Put 2 tablespoons of bicarbonate of soda, ½ cup white vinegar and 1 cup water in the pan. Bring to the boil, reduce the heat and simmer for 10–15 minutes. Drain and rinse the pan well in plenty of soapy water.

"*If 'ifs' and 'ands' were pots and pans,
there'd be no work for tinkers' hands.***"**

Charles Kingsley, 1819–1875

To stop milk burning on a saucepan

Try swirling cold water around a saucepan before heating the milk; this helps to prevent it from sticking to and burning the bottom of the pan.

Smoking oven?

If something boils over in the oven – particularly fat and oil – it will start smoking immediately. As soon as you can, sprinkle a thick layer of salt over the spillage. The smoke and smell will stop at once. Next day you'll be able to lift out the whole 'mess' with a fish slice.

" *Everyone is kneaded out of the same dough but not baked in the same oven.* **"**

Yiddish Proverb

To keep the bottom of the oven or grill pan clean

Lay a sheet of tin foil in the bottom of your oven or grill pan. Be sure to change it regularly.

To stop the smell of fried food lingering

This works, even when frying fish. Place a small bowl of white vinegar next to the cooker or fryer while you are cooking.

To remove lime scale from an electric kettle

Pour in enough white or malt vinegar to cover the element and bring it to the boil. Give the kettle a good shake to swirl the water, leave to cool and rinse thoroughly. Repeat as necessary.

To clean the microwave

Put some slices of lemon into a glass bowl.
Half fill with water and cook on high for
3 minutes. The steam will loosen the dirt and
the lemon will make the microwave smell fresh.

*" I put instant coffee in a microwave oven
and almost went back in time. "*

Stephen Wright, b.1955

" If everybody contemplates the infinite instead of fixing the drains, many of us will die of cholera."

John Rich

Taps, Drains and Gutters

To keep drains running freely

Pour ½ cup bicarbonate of soda or washing soda down the sink and then follow with 1 cup white vinegar. Leave this, without rinsing, for 15 minutes. Then pour down a kettle full of boiling water.

Avoiding blockages

Avoid pouring liquid fat or oil down your kitchen sink. If you do so, by mistake, follow it with a strong solution of hot water and washing soda.

Unblocking kitchen sinks

Bail out excess water and clear away solid debris.

✳

Use a sink plunger.

✳

If all else fails: remove the 'trap' under the sink. Remove everything from under the sink, and put a bucket or bowl under the 'trap'. Unscrew the fittings to remove a length of pipe: the water will come flooding out. If it doesn't, use an opened-out metal coat hanger to poke upwards and remove any blockage. Refit the 'trap', then flush the sink with hot water and washing soda.

To remove build up from shower heads and taps

Half fill a small plastic bag with scrunched up kitchen paper, pour in enough white vinegar to soak the paper completely. Place the bag over the shower head or tap so that the end of the nozzle is covered with vinegar paper.
Tie in place or secure with an elastic band.
Leave the bag overnight. In the morning the lime scale can be wiped away easily. If necessary, poke out any stubborn bits with a wooden cocktail stick.

To remove scum or mildew from a shower curtain

Pour 1 cup white vinegar into the fabric softener drawer. Use your normal detergent, run the cycle (40°) and re-hang the curtain immediately. It is a good idea to put some light-coloured towels in with the curtain.

Cleaning the waste disposal unit

Sprinkle a few ice cubes into the unit. Switch it
on and keep the tap running. This sharpens up
the blades. Then finish by putting some lemon
or orange peel down to make it smell fresh.

" There's no greater bliss in life than when the plumber eventually comes to unblock your drains. No writer can give that sort of pleasure."

Victoria Glendinning, b.1937

To clean taps

A small amount of shaving cream on a soft cloth is good for cleaning taps or other chrome fittings.

To clean a dirty bath

Fill it with water, add several cups of washing sods and leave for 2–3 hours or overnight. Plastic baths should not be cleaned with abrasive cleaners as it will mark them.

Brownish stains from dripping taps?

A good rub with a mixture of salt and vinegar will remove the stains easily. This mixture also works on chrome taps. Finish them by polishing with a dry cloth or chamois leather.

Clearing gutters

It makes sense to do this after the leaf fall in the autumn. Before cleaning muck out of a gutter, cover the top of the down-pipe to make sure the debris doesn't fall down the pipe. Cover with an old rag or shirt (but take care it doesn't fall down the pipe) or crumple a plastic bag into the top and secure with tape.

Emergency repairs

Heavy duty waterproof tape or duct tape is useful for emergency repairs to gutters – tape up cracks or joints to prevent water from seeping through.

"All drains lead to the ocean."

Gill in Finding Nemo

"We are all in the gutter, but some of us are looking at the stars."

Oscar Wilde, 1854–1900

"*The time to repair the roof is when the sun is shining.***"**

John Fitzgerald Kennedy, 1917–1963

To unblock an outdoor drain

Clean the obvious debris from the outdoor grill. If the drain is blocked under the grill (it will be full of water if it is), the U bend or trap underneath is probably blocked. Try pushing a length of strong but flexible wire through, such as thick but flexible electric cable.

Long cuffed rubber gloves and a little courage is the other solution! Flush the trap with plenty of water to clear it properly.

" *If you can organize your kitchen, you can organize your life.* **"**

Louis Parrish

Around the House

To make linen and clothes smell lovely

Add a few drops of your favourite toilet water to the water you pour into the steam iron.

Keep clothes wrinkle free

Do not fill your wardrobe to bursting. If you don't have much space, pack away out of season clothes in a suitcase or drawer.

To revitalize sticky zips

If a zip will not pull up easily, try rubbing it with a bar of soap or a candle. Zip it up and down a couple of times to lubricate the teeth.

To keep moths out of clothes

Mothballs will do the job, but instead you could try:

placing good, scented soap (unwrapped) among
the clothes, for example in pockets

✳

putting lavender oil on cotton wool balls and
placing them – or a dried lavender sachet –
among the clothes

✳

conkers! An old wives' tale that is
worth a go.

To close open food packets

Forget expensive, purpose-made closers,
clothes pegs will do the job just as well.

Keep the soap dish clean

Dip a cotton wool pad in baby oil and wipe over
the cleaned soap dish. The oil will repel the
water making it easier to keep the dish clean.

New jobs for old toothbrushes

Wash an old toothbrush in bleach, then rinse
and dry. They are incredibly useful for cleaning
jobs, particularly for getting into the
inaccessible crevices of artefacts
or kitchen appliances.

To cover marks on heels

Use a heavy, wide marker pen – they are
available in most colours to match shoes.
Re-apply colour as needed.

To make new soles less slippery

Rub the soles with sandpaper.

" If the shoe doesn't fit,
must we change the foot?"

Gloria Steinem, b.1935

You haven't got the right shoe polish

Spray a little furniture polish on to a rag, rub it well into the shoes and buff them to a shine. Alternatively try face or baby wipes to polish shoes and then buff them well.

Shoelaces fraying

Try dipping the ends into clear or coloured nail varnish. Leave to harden. This will stop them fraying and you will be able to thread them through the eyeholes easily.

❝ *You know you're getting old when you stoop to tie your shoelaces and wonder what else you could do while you're down there.* **❞**

George F Burns, 1896–1996

*" Children really brighten up a household –
they never turn the lights off. "*

Ralph Bus

Energy saving

Make sure that the television, computer,
dishwasher and any other similar electrical
equipment is turned off at the switch on the
receiver. If left on stand-by they consume huge
amounts of electricity – which you
have to pay for.

" *There is nothing like staying at home for real comfort.* **"**

Jane Austen 1775–1817